The Sing

Written by
Jill Atkins

Illustrated by
Pauline Reeves

Ransom

i

George was a very big, happy chef with a hairy grey chin.

People who came to George's Place enjoyed his cooking.

"I went to an excellent chef school," he laughed. "And now I have an excellent pasta machine, so my pasta is the best on the planet!"

"Oh yes," the people agreed. "You have pasta magic. Thank you, George!"

"My pleasure!" laughed George. "I can boil it, fry it, roast it … I can even cook it with my eyes shut!"

"You are a treasure!" the people told him.

But the main thing people enjoyed about George was his singing.

He sang happily as he went to the gym.

He sang loudly as he rode his bike to work.

He sang merrily as he cooked his prize-winning pasta and served it to his customers.

Because of this, George was a fantastic success – so he made a lot of money.

But one day, as George rode along an icy road, his bike skidded and he fell off. Tears streamed from his eyes.

"Ow!" he moaned. "I have a headache, but I must cook my pasta because I must serve my customers. I cannot let them go hungry."

So he got up and rode back to George's Place.

George cooked his pasta and served it to his customers, but this time he did not sing.

The customers sat in George's Place and munched on the pasta.

"This is not the same as usual," said one man.

The next day was the same. The pasta was not as good as usual.

Soon, the customers stopped eating at George's Place.

Then one day, George met one of his customers in the street.

"Why did you stop singing?" asked the man.

"It was shock. I fell off my bike," said George. "Now I cannot sing and so my pasta is no good."

"Why don't you make a big pasta parcel?" asked the man. "People might come and try it."

So George took the man's advice. And when the pasta was cooked, he placed it outside in the sun. The pasta parcel swelled up, until …

Bang!

George landed on his bottom as the pasta parcel burst into a hundred bits.

What a shock!

Then suddenly, a new sound resounded round the town.

It was the sound of George singing.

"Hooray!" shouted the crowd. "The old George is back."

And they all flocked into George's Place for dinner.

And George has not stopped singing since!